Jonathan branch is the American author of some of American favorite short self-published children's books. He began writing poetry and teaching Pre algebra at the age of 18. He is a celebrated and established author and awarded writer by many. His book shows display his works at Barnes and noble, local book stores and toy stores in Princeton, New Jersey and in Hopewell, Virginia. Jonathan branch is a former firefighter and rescue squad member. He is also up for the African American world record for the title of most children's books. He speaks 3 languages and teaches GED courses online for displaced individuals who look up to him for guidance. He has spoken on the radio and has given many speeches all over the states. He has received numerous awards including the prudential youth leadership award, awards from Washington dc and was the former vice president of toast masters. Currently he is working on medical patents for children with physical therapy and bone cancer equipment for pediatric patients.

Welcome to Childbranch Books

We have written the best action and adventure books for children for years. So sit back and get ready to travel far away to rescue a princess or fight a dragon ....

Enjoy the magic ....

To all the parents that love to read our books at night to your lovely children......

Thank You

We will continue our great work in pursiut of great accomplishments. Our illustrators are from Italy, London and the Philippines. We have 235 books to write so keep reading ......

Sandy walked up to the front of the classroom and started to give her speech on science. It would be a big speech for her today.

"In nature, the cow eats the grass that doesn't need to be planted. The grass is given light by the sun which also feeds the corn.

The cycle of sunlight to the plants to the cows has existed for hundreds of years."

"This is the ocean and in it everybody's hungry

The shark eats the
barracuda. The
barracuda eats the fish
and the fish eats the
sea plankton."

"Solar panels are used in everyday life from powering our homes to helping Nasa conserve energy. They cost us less and protect the environment."

"In Africa, people use sunlight to clean their water. Sunlight is very powerful when focused with a mirror. It can clean particles and remove harmful germs."

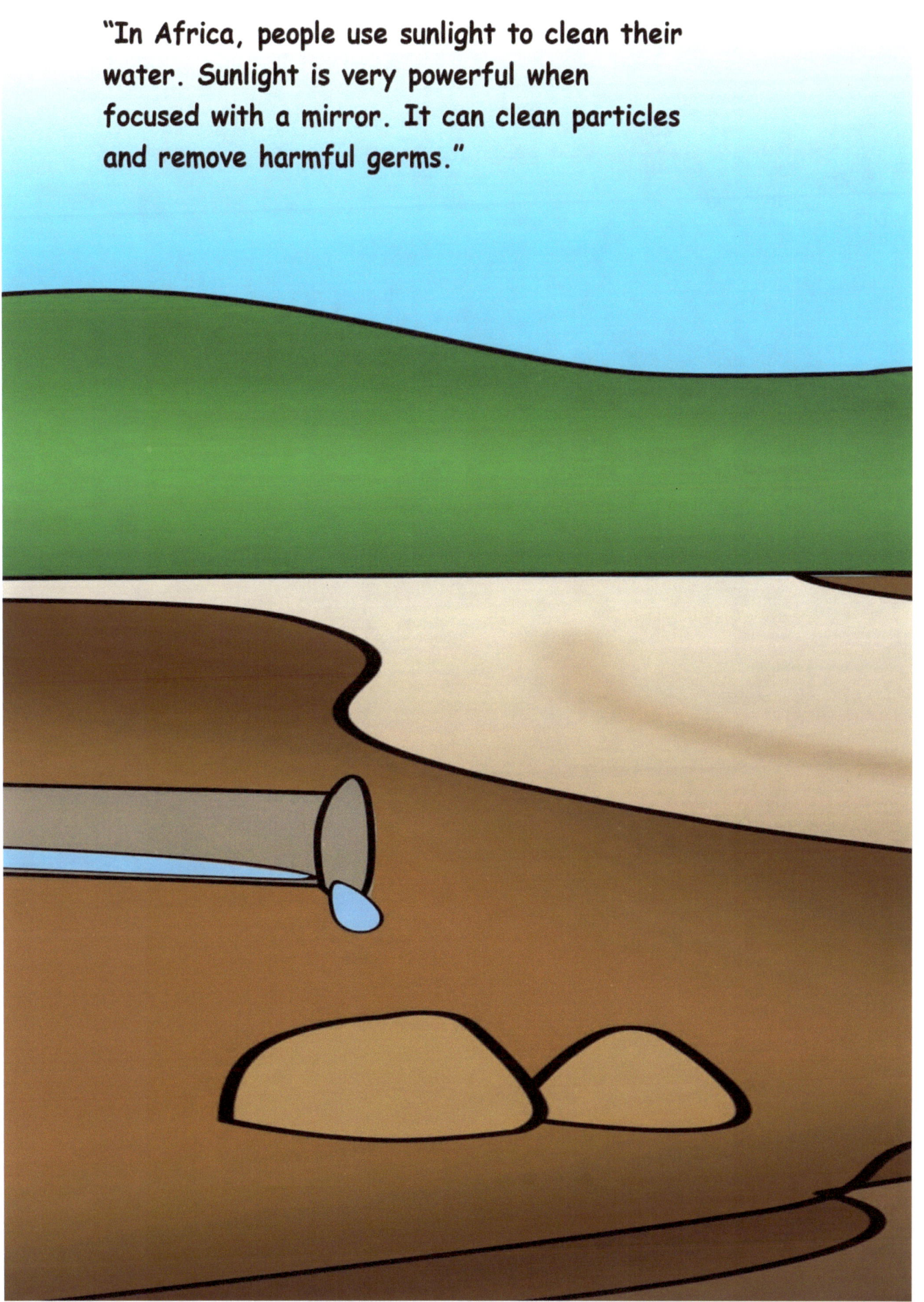

"Our world is protected by a special magnetic field. The field stops powerful sunlight and rocks from hitting us and keeps bad radiation away."

"An astronaut has to wear a special suit to protect him from space. He need oxygen to breathe and gets it from a tube connected to the space shuttle to make sure he doesn't float away."

"Our planets orbit the sun in circles. We live in a big place called the solar system."

"This is our galaxy that we live in. NASA says there are aliens in there, possibly flying around. But I think our New Jersey taxes will keep them away for a few hundred years."

"Man has been fighting with nature for thousands of years. From catching lions to fighting old age. We constantly try to improve ourselves to battle the odds whatever comes our way."

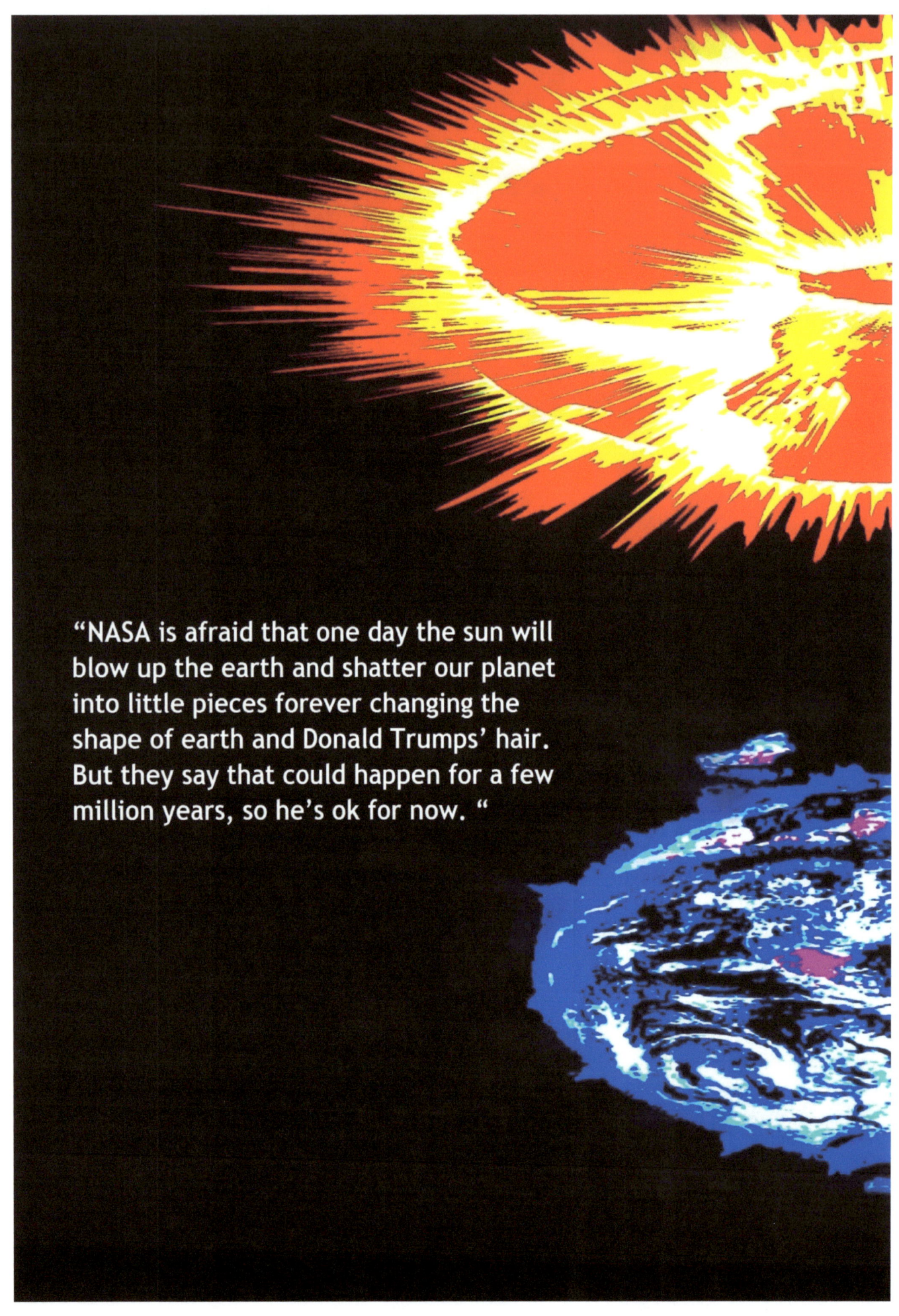

"NASA is afraid that one day the sun will blow up the earth and shatter our planet into little pieces forever changing the shape of earth and Donald Trumps' hair. But they say that could happen for a few million years, so he's ok for now. "

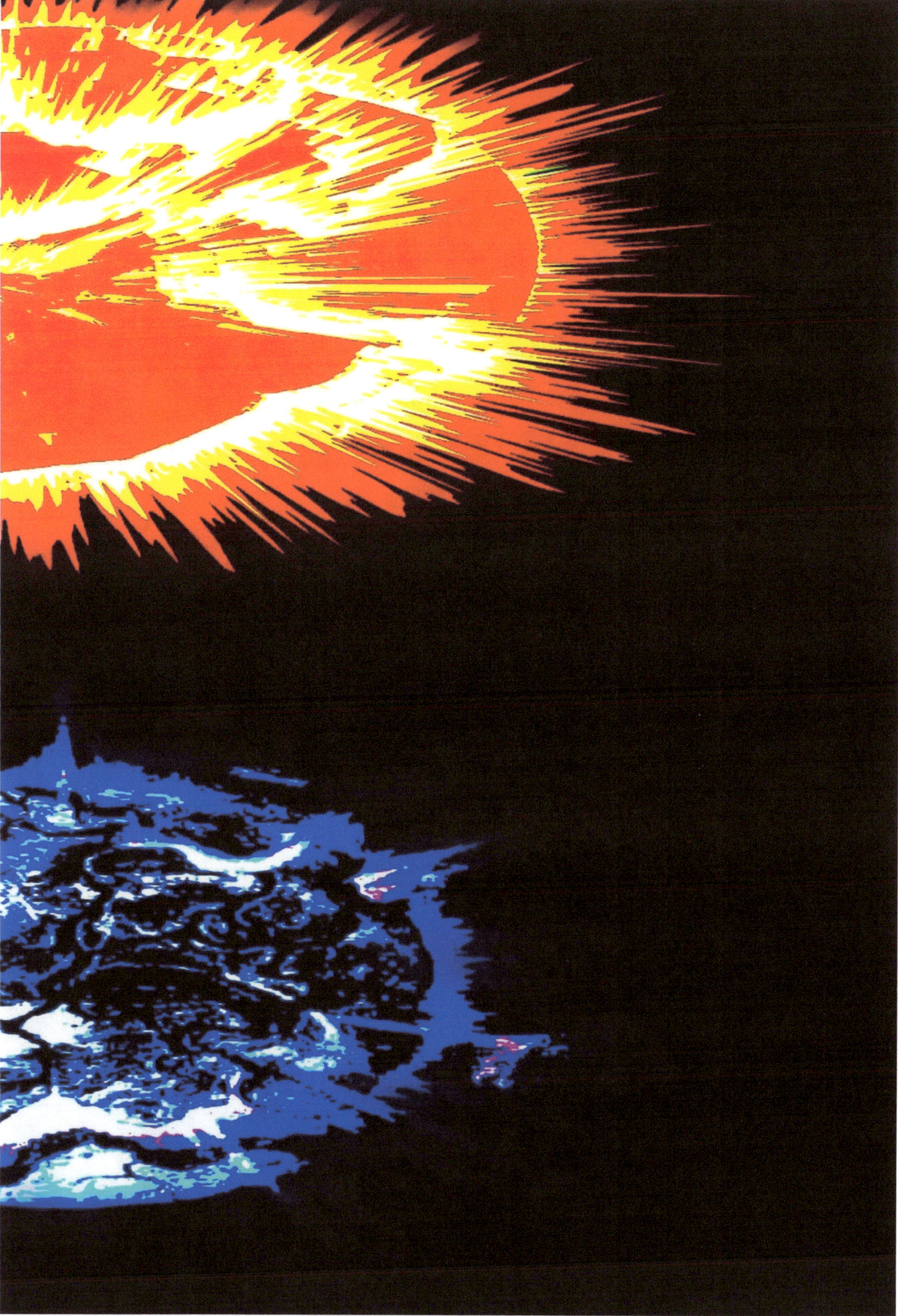

"We all must learn to protect our planet and preserve what we have left. This is the only planet that we have and, if we can't live with ourselves and over tax others, this will be a miserable planet."

"However we could worry about the aliens that do abduct us from time to time. People in Alaska claim that aliens abduct them and take them away for years at a time. The government has been investigating such claims but reminds its civilians to still pay their taxes."

"Thank you everyone, that concludes the end of my glorious presentation."

We would like to take the
time to thank our amazing
illustrators and editors

Edward Kos
Raymond Ariola
Amy foster
Clizia Brozzesi
Jhoiye Mendoza
Michele Paoluccci

Raymond Ariola passed away
during the philippines storm.
We will miss him greatly!

More Spectacular Books on the Way !!

 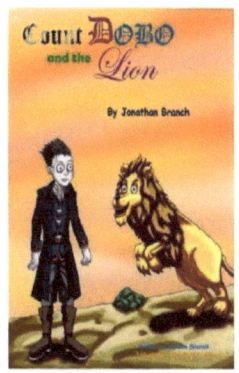  

   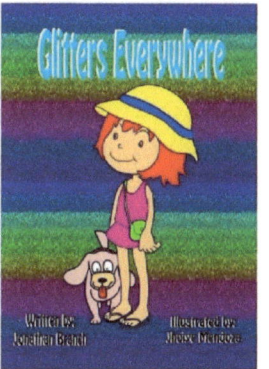

  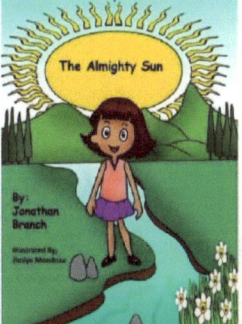 

 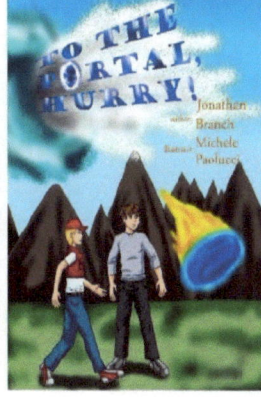